Bird Day

by Charles Almanzo Babcock

AUTHOR'S NOTE

The aim of this book is to assist school children in the accurate study of a few birds. It is believed that if this be attained, further study of birds will take care of itself.

Thanks are due the Audubon Society, ornithologists, educators, and legislators, for the generous approbation and assistance which they have given the Bird Day movement.

Special thanks are due the Department of Agriculture for permission to use the illustrations in this volume. Those on pages 65, 67, 69, 71, 73, 75, 77, 79, 85, 87, 89, 93, and 95 are printed from electrotypes from the original illustrations appearing in "Farmer's Bulletin," No. 54. Those on pages 81 and 83 are from the Yearbook of the Department for 1899, and that on page 91 from the Yearbook for 1898. All these publications are issued by the Department.

CONTENTS

BIRD DAY

HOW TO PREPARE FOR IT

I

HISTORY OF THE MOVEMENT FOR "BIRD DAY"

In the spring of 1894 the writer's attention was attracted to the interest of the children in that part of their nature study which related to birds. Their descriptions of the appearance and habits of the birds they had observed were given with evident pleasure. They had a strong desire to tell what they had seen, not in the spirit of rivalry, but with the wish of adding to the knowledge of a subject in which all were equally interested.

It was thought that this work would be done with even more effectiveness if a day were appointed to be celebrated as "Bird Day." With the hope of making a memorable occasion of the day for those taking part in it, several of the noted friends of birds were asked to write something to the children, and to give their opinion of the introduction of "Bird Day" into the schools.

Secretary J. Sterling Morton, the father of "Arbor Day," responded with the following earnest letter, which was at once given to the public through Washington dispatches, and later was sent out from the Department of Agriculture, in circular No. 17:--

WASHINGTON, D. C., April 23, 1894.

MR. C. A. BABCOCK, SUPERINTENDENT OF SCHOOLS, OIL CITY, PA.

Dear Sir,--Your proposition to establish a "Bird Day" on the same general plan as "Arbor Day," has my cordial approval.

Such a movement can hardly fail to promote the development of a healthy public sentiment toward our native birds, favoring their preservation and increase. If directed toward this end, and not to the encouragement of the importation of foreign species, it is sure to meet the approval of the American people.

It is a melancholy fact that among the enemies of our birds two of the most destructive and relentless are our women and our boys. The love of feather ornamentation so heartlessly persisted in by thousands of women, and the mania for collecting eggs and killing birds so deeply rooted in our boys, are legacies of barbarism inherited from our savage ancestry. The number of beautiful and useful birds annually slaughtered for bonnet trimmings runs up into the hundreds of thousands, and threatens, if it has not already accomplished, the extermination of some of the rarer species. The insidious egg-hunting and pea-shooting proclivities of the small boy are hardly less widespread and destructive. It matters little which of the two agencies is the more fatal, since neither is productive of any good. One looks to the gratification of a shallow vanity, the other to the gratification of a cruel instinct and an expenditure of boyish energy that might be profitably diverted into other channels. The evil is one against which legislation can be only palliative and of local efficiency. Public sentiment, on the other hand, if properly fostered in the schools, would gain force with the growth and development of our boys and girls, and would become a hundredfold more potent than any law enacted by the State or Congress. I believe such a sentiment can be developed, so strong and so universal that a respectable woman will be ashamed to be seen with the wing of a wild bird on her bonnet, and an honest boy will be ashamed to own that he ever robbed a nest or wantonly took the life of a bird.

Birds are of inestimable value to mankind. Without their unremitting services our gardens and fields would be laid waste by insect pests. But we owe them a greater debt even than this, for the study of birds tends to develop some of the best attributes and impulses of our natures. Among them we find examples of generosity, unselfish devotion, of the love of mother for offspring, and other estimable qualities. Their industry, patience, and ingenuity excite our admiration; their songs inspire us with a love of music and poetry; their beautiful plumages and graceful manners appeal to our aesthetic sense; their long migrations to distant lands stimulate our imaginations and tempt us to inquire into the causes of these periodic movements; and finally, the endless modifications of form and habits by which they are enabled to live under most diverse conditions of food and climate--on land and at sea--invite the student of nature into inexhaustible fields of pleasurable research.

The cause of bird protection is one that appeals to the best side of our natures. Let us yield to the appeal. Let us have a Bird Day--a day set apart from all the other days of the year to tell the children about the birds. But we must not stop here. We should strive continually to develop and intensify the sentiment of bird protection, not alone for the sake of preserving the birds, but also for the sake of replacing as far as possible the barbaric impulses inherent in child nature by the nobler impulses and aspirations that should characterize advanced civilization.

Respectfully,

J. STERLING MORTON,

Secretary of Agriculture.

Other friends of the birds responded cordially to the request, as will be seen by the following letters:--

WEST PARK, N. Y., April 22, 1894.

Dear Sir,--In response to yours of the seventeenth, I enclose a few notes about birds to be read upon your "Bird Day"--just an item or two to stimulate the curiosity of the young people. The idea is a good one, and I hope you may succeed in starting a movement that may extend to all the schools of the country.

Very truly yours,

JOHN BURROUGHS.

628 HANCOCK STREET, BROOKLYN, N. Y., April 25, 1894.

MR. C. A. BABCOCK.

Dear Sir,--Yours of the nineteenth is received. I am delighted to know that your school children are to have a "Bird Day." I wish I could be there to tell them something of the delight of getting acquainted with their little brothers in feathers; how much more interesting they are when alive and doing all sorts of quaint and charming things than when dead and made into "skins" or stuffed; and how much greater is the pleasure of watching them to see how they live, where they get their dinner, how they take care of themselves, than of killing them, or hurting them, or even just driving them away. If the boys and girls only try keeping still and watching birds to see what they will do, I am sure no boy will ever again want to throw a stone at one, and no girl ever to have a dead bird on her hat.

Very truly yours,

OLIVE THORNE MILLER.

CLINTON, April 30, 1894.

My Dear Sir,--It strikes me that your idea is a particularly happy one. Should you institute a "Bird Day," the feathered tribe ought to furnish music for the occasion. A chorus of robins and thrushes and a few other songsters would be more appropriate than an orchestra. With thanks for your cordial good wishes, I am,

Yours faithfully,

CLINTON SCOLLARD.

From the Department of Public Instruction of Pennsylvania this encouraging letter was received:--
HARRISBURG, April 27, 1894.

SUPERINTENDENT C. A. BABCOCK.

Dear Sir,--In your plan to inaugurate a "Bird Day" you have struck a capital idea. When in the name of agriculture a scalp act can be passed resulting in a year and a half in the payment of $75,000 by the county treasuries of Pennsylvania for the destruction of birds that were subsequently proved to belong to the feathered friends of the farmer, it is high time to make our pupils acquainted with the habits and ways of the feathered tribes. Some birds remain with us the whole year, others are summer sojourners, still others are only transient visitors. How much of the beauty of our environment is lost by those who never listen to the music of the birds and never see the richness of their plumage!

May success attend you in carrying out your new idea of a "Bird Day."

Very truly yours,

NATHAN C. SCHAEFFER,

Superintendent of Public Instruction.

Bradford Torrey gives an additional title to the day, showing his appreciation of it:--

WELLESLEY HILLS, MASS., April 21, 1894.

Dear Mr. Babcock,--Your young people are to be congratulated. "Bird Day" is something new to me--a new saints' day in my calendar, so to speak. The thought is so pleasing to me that I wish you had given me its date, so that in spirit I might observe it with you. Tell your pupils that to cultivate an acquaintance with things out of doors--flowers, trees, rocks, but especially animate creatures, and best of all, birds--is one of the surest ways of laying up happiness for themselves; and laying up happiness is even better than laying up money, though I am so old-fashioned a body and so true a Yankee as to believe in that also.

All the naturalists I have known have been men of sunny temper. Let your boys and girls cultivate their eyes and ears, and their hearts and minds as well, by the study of living birds, their comings and goings, their songs and their ways; let them learn to find out things for themselves; to know the difference between guess-work and knowledge; and they will thank you as long as they live for having encouraged them in so good a cause. With all good wishes for the success of your first "Bird Day"--and many to come after it,

Very truly yours,

BRADFORD TORREY.

The first observance of "Bird Day," May 4, 1894, is briefly set forth in the following paragraph from the New England Journal of Education:--

The day was observed in the Oil City schools with a degree of enthusiasm which was good to see. The amount of information about birds that was collected by the children was simply amazing. Original compositions were read, informal discussions were held, talks by teachers were given, and the birds in literature were not forgotten or overlooked. The interest was not confined to the children, one gentleman surprising the classes in which his children celebrated the day by presenting to them artistic programs of the exercises.

It seems to those interested that the idea simply needs to be made known to meet with a warm welcome, akin to that with which we greet our first robin or song sparrow in the spring.

II

THE VALUE OF BIRDS

Probably few people understand the value of birds or comprehend how closely and yet how extensively their lives are interwoven with other forms of life. The general sentiment in regard to them, at the best, has been that they are harmless, even interesting and beautiful creatures; but the idea that they are one of the most important classes of creation, a class upon which the existence of many other classes depends, has never been widely prevalent. Suppose we were asked which is of more use to man, the fishes of our waters or the birds of our forests and fields? Many of us would unhesitatingly answer in favor of the fishes.

If all of these denizens of the rivers, lakes, and seas should be destroyed, it would be a stupendous calamity. Mankind would universally deplore it; and if the nations of the world should, at any time, become convinced that such a thing might occur, how quickly they would take all possible means to prevent it! All civilized people now have laws to preserve this food supply and are making expensive and laborious efforts to increase it. Any one who should destroy thousands of tons of these edible swimmers, simply for their heads and tails, or fins and scales, would be regarded as a dangerous person. But if our supposition were realized, if every fin and gill were to disappear from the waters of the globe, what would be the result? A misfortune, truly, for the fins represent a large part of the world's supply of food, and this loss would be felt more deeply as time went on, because the ocean will not raise its rent, however crowded may be the population of its shores. The effort to secure the fish might be applied, however, in other directions and be equally remunerative. Harvest would still follow seedtime; the gold of autumn still reward the shallow mines of spring.

But suppose we were forced to the dreadful alternative of choosing between the birds and the quadrupeds, again, the most of us would probably decide against the birds. If the four-footed beasts should disappear from the earth, it would be a much greater disaster than the destruction of the fishes. A much larger fraction of the food supply would be lost; while many of these animals contribute to man's comfort and necessities in almost innumerable ways. Most nations have learned to cherish their friends with hoofs and horns, and even some of those with claws. Cruelty to animals is now generally forbidden by law; and their wanton destruction would be regarded with horror. No one would be permitted to slaughter large numbers of them because he might wish to sell their horns or ears or the tips of their tails.

By the departure of the quadrupeds the life of man would be rendered much more difficult, but would still be possible. From fish and fowl he could obtain a supply of meat limited in variety, yet sufficient for his needs. The treasures of the vegetable world would still be his, though he would miss the help of his animal allies in securing them; but his ingenuity would help him to supply this loss, in part, at least.

Consider now what would be the effect of the total destruction of birds. Birds are nature's check to the amazing power of insects to increase. If insect life were allowed free course, it would soon overpower vegetation; and plant life--and, therefore, animal life, including that of man--would be impossible upon this globe. This is an astounding conclusion, but it is sustained by the judgment of every man of science who has investigated the subject. How long could the ravages of insects be stayed were the birds gone? We should have to depend upon a few predaceous beetles, the bats, and upon the sprayers and squirtguns which throw insecticides. Think of the 鎧thetic loss in substituting these agencies for the "sweet spirits" of the wood and field! Besides not being musical or charming in action, they would not prove efficient. Birds are therefore essential to the life of man.

Their preservation is not merely a matter of sentiment, or of education in that high and fine feeling, kindness to all living things. It has a utilitarian side of vast extent, as broad as our boundless fields and our orchards' sweep. The birds are nature's guarantee that the reign of the crawlers and spinners shall not become universal. The "plague of locusts" shall be upon those who sin against them.

III

THE DESTRUCTION OF BIRDS

From almost all sections of the country comes the plaint that the song birds are fast disappearing. Less and less numerous are the yearly visitations of the thrushes, warblers, song sparrows, orioles, and the others whose habits have been so delightful and whose music has been so cheering to their open-eyed and open-hearted friends. Many, who when listening to the hymn-like cadences of the wood thrush have felt that the place was holy ground, are now keenly regretting that this vesper song is so rare; the honest sweetness of the song sparrow mingles with the coarser sounds less often in the accustomed places. Not many now find "the meadows spattered all over with music" by the bobolink, as Thoreau did.

John Burroughs says that the bluebird is almost extinct in his section of country. The writer, though a frequent visitor to the fields and woods, has succeeded in seeing only one pair of these beautiful birds in two seasons, where they were abundant a few years ago, when almost every orchard bore a good crop of them. A friend who is a good observer has had the same experience. A careful exploration of the country within a radius of five miles resulted in the discovery of only two pairs of bobolinks, having their nests luckily in the same field. The males sang together in friendly rivalry. The sparkling, tinkling notes seemed to come in a rippling tumble, two or three at a time, from each throat. Each started his song with his feet barely touching his perch, his body quivering, his wings half extended, as if he were almost supported by the upward flow of his melody. After circular flights he alighted first upon one frail, swinging perch, then upon another, the wonderful sounds not ceasing, as if he were tracing magic rings of song round his home, and making them thick in places. It was a musical embodiment of the love of life and of its joyousness.

The brown thrush is also absent from places where once there were many. A farmer in this neighborhood states that a few years ago the treetops near his house seemed to be filled with these fine singers. Now he hears only one or two during the season. Last May the writer found three nests at least a mile apart, but they were destroyed before the time of hatching, and the birds went about silent as if brooding upon their trouble. It is doubtful if they will build next season in that vicinity. No doubt the clearing away of the forests and the settling up of the country are responsible for the scarcity of the birds in part, but only in part. If they were let alone, many of the most interesting and useful birds would build near even our city homes, and our gardens and fields would again become populous with them.

The wearing of feathers and the skins of birds for ornament is the chief cause of the final flight of many of our songsters. It is stated that a London dealer received at one time more than thirty thousand dead humming birds. Not only brightly colored birds, but any small birds, by means of dyes, may come at last to such base uses. It is estimated by some of the Audubon societies that ten million birds were used in this country in one season. All these bodies, which are used to make "beauty much more beauteous seem," are steeped in arsenical solutions to prevent their becoming as offensive to the nostrils of their wearers as they are to the eyes of bird lovers.

The use of dead birds for adornment is a constant object lesson in cruelty, a declaration louder than any words that a bird's life is not to be respected. It is currently reported that a million bobolinks were destroyed in Pennsylvania alone last year to satisfy the demand of the milliners. If this "garniture of death" is in good taste, then our North American Indian in his war paint and feathers was far ahead of his time.

Let us hope that some oracle of fashion will decree that if the remains of animals must be used for adornment, the skins of mice and rats shall be offered up. Their office seems to be principally that of scavengers, and their gradual but certain extinction would not matter if the Christian nations should become, pari passu, more cleanly. The squirrel could also be used effectively, mounted as if half flying, with his hind feet fastened to the velvet pedestal, or sitting upon his haunches with a nut between his fore paws. The squirrel's main concern seems to be to prevent the undue extension of the nut-bearing trees--an office man has already well taken upon himself--and besides, he destroys fruit, injures trees, and is a great enemy of birds. His gradual extinction would be tolerated by a civilized nation.

All these things may take the hues of the rainbow and are capable of infinite variety of arrangement. There certainly seems to be no good reason why in a few years some combination of them may not be considered as effective as a row of dead humming birds. The world may be saved in this way from presenting a spectacle that should excite the pity of gods and men--the spectacle of the destruction of one of the most beautiful, the most harmless, and the most useful classes of creation, at the command of the senseless whims of fashion.

Then, too, the sportsmen's guns and the small boys' slings and shooters of various sorts are constantly bringing down numbers of the feathered songsters. In many parts of our country men and boys roam the fields, shooting at every bird they see, and their action is tacitly approved by the community. This survival of the barbarous instinct to kill is condoned as "sport." If these people were to spend this time in following the birds with opera glass and notebook to study them, they might not be so readily understood--they might even be taken for mild lunatics, so utterly is public sentiment perverted on this subject.

A little consideration shows this destruction to be more disastrous than at first appears. According to the latest biological science, every species of animals must have long ago reached the limit beyond which it could not greatly increase its numbers. However great its tendency to increase might be, its natural obstacles and enemies would increase in like proportions till at last the two would balance each other, and there could be no further increase in the number of individuals of that species. All classes of animals in a state of nature must have reached this balanced condition generations ago. This is true of the birds. Their natural enemies are capable of preventing their increase; that is, they can and do destroy every year as many as are hatched that year. Now if man be added as a new destructive agency, the old enemies, being still able to destroy as many as before, will soon sweep them out of existence. Warnings have been sent out by the United States Department of Biology that several species of birds are already close to extinction. We know that this is true of the passenger pigeon. This bird used to come North in flocks so extensive as sometimes to obscure the sun, like a large, thick cloud. Now they come no more. Italy is practically songless, we are told.

If man would right the wrong that he has done, he must not only stop destroying the birds, but he must take all possible means to preserve them and to protect them from their natural foes.

Laws for bird protection have been passed in many of our states; but these have been found effective only where they were not needed. They are, however, right, and will help in the development of correct sentiment. What is most needed is knowledge of the birds themselves, their modes of life, their curious ways, and their relations to the scheme of things. To know a bird is to love him. Birds are beautiful and interesting objects of study, and make appeals to children that are responded to with delight.

Children love intensely the forms of nature--the clouds, the trees, the flowers, the animals--all of the great beautiful world outside of themselves, and it is their impulse to become acquainted with this world; for this they feel enthusiasm and love. Marjorie Fleming, the little playmate of Scott, who at the age of six could recite passages from Shakespeare and Burns so that the great bard would sob like a child or shout with laughter, may be taken as the universal voice of childhood. She writes in her diary, "I am going to a delightful place where there is ducks, cocks, hens, bubblejacks, two dogs, two cats and swine which is delightful." In another place she says, "Braehead is extremely pleasant to me by the company of swine, geese, cocks, etc., and they are the delight of my soul."

The waste of time in our public schools has been commented upon and some of the causes have been pointed out; but is not the chief reason the fact that much of the work of the school is unrelated to the world of the child? At least the child does not see the connection. He leaves at the threshold the things which he loves and desires intensely to investigate, and begins his intellectual development with abstractions, with "the three R's." It is said that teachers cannot succeed unless they love their work. How can we expect children to succeed and not waste time, not become disheartened at work that, so far as they can discover, has little more relation to their interests than to the mountains of the moon?

We look to nature study to supply the missing links between the child's life and his school work; to afford opportunities for the interested observation of things, and to furnish a strong impulse toward expression. It has been well said that the best result of the primary schools is the power to use correctly one's own language. The chief obstacle in the development of this power is the want of an impulse to express. What can afford a stronger tendency to describe than the attempt to report observations that have been made with interest, even with delight?

IV

PLAN OF STUDY

Begin as soon after the first of January as possible. Assign two periods a week of from ten to twenty minutes each for bird study in the school. Continue the work during these periods until after the celebration of Bird Day in May.

If no other bird is to be found, the English sparrow will answer. Place the following questions upon the blackboard:--

THE ENGLISH SPARROW

How long is this bird from the tip of its beak to the end of its tail?

What is the color of its head? Of its throat? Of its breast? Of the underparts of its body? Of its back? Of its wings?

What is the length, shape, and color of its bill?

What is the color of its legs and feet? How many toes upon each foot, and which way do they point? Does it walk, hop, or run upon the ground? Is its tail square, or notched? Is its flight even and steady, or bounding? What is the difference in appearance between the male and female?

The children should be directed to answer these questions from their own observation, at the next period of study. For the lowest grades two or three questions will be enough for the first attempt, and even then the variety of answers will be surprising.

No other questions should be taken until the first are answered correctly.

The teacher should have an opera glass or a small field glass with which to make her own observations. It is obvious that the more glasses there are among the children, the better. It is advisable for the teacher to make short excursions with the children to the streets to assist them in answering these questions. These can be made at the close of school. As a preparation, have some crumbs or seeds scattered where the birds have been seen.

Continue work with these questions until each one can give a reasonably accurate description of the appearance of the bird and of its movements. Have the older pupils write this. It will make a good language lesson.

The next questions should have reference to the life and characteristics of the bird. What does it eat? Put out crumbs or scraps of meat and see if the bird will eat them. What sounds does the bird make? Does it sing? Imitate as many of its sounds as you can. Determine from its actions what its disposition is. For example--Is it courageous? Is it quarrelsome? Is it inclined to fight? Is it selfish?

Frequently a single incident in a bird's life will furnish an answer to several of these questions. Two sparrows were seen attempting to take possession of the same straw. Each held firmly to his end of the straw. A regular tug of war ensued. They pulled one another about for some time on the top of an awning, and finally, becoming tired of this, they dropped the straw and furiously attacked each other. They fought with beak and claw, paying no attention to the spectators, and fell exhausted to the sidewalk, where they lay upon their backs until able to hop slowly away from each other. It was some little time before they recovered strength to fly in opposite directions, conquering and unconquered.

Early in March advise the children to watch the direction of the sparrows' flight. They will discover that some of them are carrying straws or feathers or other material for nest building. Notice the position and style of these nests. Those built early in the season are always in protected places, under the eaves of houses or in holes in trees or in bird boxes. Some of those built later are in exposed places, clumsy affairs, but well thatched with straw, having an entrance on one side. This nest building may be watched during the entire season, for the English sparrow raises more broods than any other of our birds.

The interpretation of the actions which indicate any of a bird's characteristics is a valuable part of the study on account of its exercise of the imagination and the reason.

A plan similar to the foregoing should be followed with each bird that is studied. With almost all other birds the study will be far more interesting. The English sparrow may be considered as the A B C of birds in his appearance and in the kind of life he leads. He is therefore a good subject to begin with. But even he will be found to exhibit unexpected individuality.

After a few days of this study, or at least before the spring birds begin to arrive, direct the children to try the following experiments. Scatter crumbs where they may be seen from the windows. Nail cups in the trees containing sugar and water, and others containing seeds. Nail up a bone or two, and a piece of suet as large as your two hands. This last will be relished by the birds, for it provides the kind of food most needed in cold weather.

Watch carefully the birds that are attracted by the food. After feeding awhile they will become quite tame and may be closely approached. Write a description of each bird upon the plan used for the English sparrow. Encourage the children to add any observations of their own which throw light upon the habits and character of the birds, since one object of this study is the development of right feeling toward them.

Among the first to arrive will probably be the blue jay, chickadee, or black-capped titmouse, and one or more of the woodpeckers. These all show individual character and are well worth studying.

The blue jay by his striking appearance and outlandish voice challenges attention. He will be found to possess some gentlemanly traits. To illustrate, a number of blue jays were seen taking turns, waiting in line, to feed upon a bone where there was room for only one at a time. There was no scramble, no hurrying of the one who was eating. The blue jay is a most devoted parent, though not considered a good citizen by other birds. Contrary to the usual belief, he has a beautiful song. It is sweet and low and almost as varied as the catbird's, and can be heard only a short distance. It has a reminiscent character, as if he were thinking of past joys.

The black-capped titmouse or the chickadee is noticeable for his sprightliness and cheeriness, and for his trim, tailor-made appearance. Emerson's poem worthily celebrates his brave spirit. He flits around a limb and clings to it with his head up or down, with his feet up or down, as if his movements were not physical exertions, but mental efforts. His simple little song rings out at all hours of the coldest day.

The woodpecker gives himself freely to study. One winter we frequently counted from twelve to fourteen children standing under the tree on which a little sapsucker was at work. The upturned faces of the children did not disturb him at all, although he was only a little above their heads. He drilled away as if his work in the world was the work which must be done. A downy woodpecker with a slightly wounded wing was brought into one of our schoolrooms, where he lived contentedly for several days, pecking a dead treetop, which the boys brought in for him after a good deal of thought and several excursions. The only food he seemed to like was sweetened water, although the children brought him a great variety to choose from. No visitor to a schoolroom ever produced a better effect. His presence, instead of interfering with the regular order, pleased the children, and they did their work even better than usual. When his wing was healed he was dismissed from school through the window, and his flight to a neighboring treetop was anxiously watched.

Upon many other occasions wounded birds have been brought into our schools. Some recovered and others died, but each visit was an epoch in the life of the school.

The other birds most likely to visit this feast during January are the flicker, crow, purple finch, song sparrow, white-breasted nuthatch, snow-flake; American crossbill, white-throated sparrow, tree sparrow, junco, winter wren, golden-crowned kinglet, brown creeper, and even the solitary robin. The sparrow hawk and the sharp-shinned hawk may visit the vicinity to feed upon the other feeders. On the first of January I saw a sparrow hawk sitting on the spire of a church in the heart of a city of eighteen thousand people. After selecting a victim from the sparrows on the street below, he calmly spread his wings and pounced upon him, or with no effort at concealment chased the bird whose flight was nearest.

A female sparrow hawk wintered in the eaves of an apartment house in Morningside Park, New York City. English sparrow was its principal diet, and every morning and afternoon an observer might have seen the hawk soar to the park grounds on its hunting trips.

A few years ago a sharp-shinned hawk visited our yard. Apparently he lived upon the sparrows there for several days. There was no skill in his hunting or effort to take the game unawares. When he wanted a bird he simply left his perch and captured it by speed of wing. His ease of flight was remarkable; as a little boy said, "He just opened his wings and sailed away." He stayed until the sparrows left the neighborhood.

As the season advances the birds will come in greater numbers. On the first of April a little girl in one of our schools had identified and described seventeen different species of birds which she had seen in her yard. The same child fed a family of chipping sparrows; they became so tame that they would come to meet her when she came with crumbs, and would pick them up even when they dropped close to her feet. The next year this family evidently came again and raised another brood and brought them along to be fed, for seven and sometimes eight would come when she called. The English sparrow came also, and the little maid drove them away without the chippies being disturbed. A boy from one of our schools was even more fortunate. In his yard were a number of trees in which ample provision had been made for the birds. Late in April, with other kinds a pair of scarlet tanagers and a pair of rose-breasted grosbeaks visited the trees. These stayed and soon seemed to feel quite at home. To the great delight of their neighbors, the house-dwellers, they built their nests, the grosbeaks in a tree near one side of the porch, the tanagers in one near the opposite side. They became so friendly that sometimes when the boy came out upon the porch and played softly on a mouth organ, the grosbeak's silvery warble and the tanager's loud, clear voice joined him.

Brief written descriptions should be made by the pupils, similar to the following:--

BLUEBIRD.--Length, six and a half inches; extent of wings, about twelve inches; color, back, azure blue; throat, breast, and sides, dull crimson; underpart, white; bill and legs, blackish; eye, brown; arrives early in March; leaves in late November. Song, soft and pleasing warble; sings both in flight and at rest; nests in holes of trees or posts, or in bird houses.

CHICKADEE.--Length, about five and a half inches; extent of wings, about eight inches; legs, bluish gray; bill, black; back, brownish gray; throat, chin, and top of head, black; sides of head, white; underparts, whitish; wing and tail feathers margined with white; nests in holes in trees and stumps. The common name arises from their familiar note of "chic-a-dee-dee."

CATBIRD.--Length, nine inches; extent of wings, eleven and a half inches; bill and feet, black; eye, brown; color, slate color, somewhat lighter beneath; top of head and tail, black; reddish under the wings; arrives in May, leaves in October; nests in bushes; lives in gardens and woodside thickets; has a sharp cry not unlike the mewing of a cat, but is a gifted songster.

MEADOW LARK.--Length, about ten and a half inches; extent of wings, about sixteen and a half inches; female is smaller; body, thick and stout; legs, large; hind toe reaches out beyond the tail, its claw twice as long as the middle one; bill, brown, lighter at the base, dark towards the point; feet and legs, light brown; throat, breast, and edge of wing, bright yellow; breast with a large black crescent; nests on the ground in the open field; clumsy in flight and in walking; song, a plaintive whistle; arrives in March, leaves in October.

BARN SWALLOW.--Length, six and three fourths inches; spread of wings, twelve and a half inches; bill, black; legs and feet, light brown; color, upper parts glossy steel blue; tail, very deeply forked, outer tail feathers much longer and narrower than the others; forehead, chin, and throat, deep chestnut; rest of the underparts lighter; nests usually in barns.

WOOD THRUSH.--Length, eight inches; spread of wings, thirteen inches; legs and feet, flesh-colored; bill, blackish, lighter at base; upper parts cinnamon brown, brightest on top of the head, and shading into olive near the tail; lower parts white and marked with roundish, dusky spots; arrives the first of May, leaves in October. Song consists of sweet, ringing, bell-like notes.

Later these outlines should be expanded into free descriptions, containing all that the pupil has learned about the bird, his habits, his character, and his life.

Each school should aim to possess a bird manual, for the identification of the species. The following are recommended as sufficient for the purpose: "Birds of the United States," by A. C. Apgar; "Birds of Eastern North America," by Frank M. Chapman; "Bird Craft," by Mabel Osgood Wright; "Birds of Pennsylvania," second edition, by Warren (this may possibly be obtained at second-hand bookstores); "Our Common Birds and How to Know Them," by Grant. The report of your own state upon birds, if there is one, will also furnish valuable information.

V

FURTHER SUGGESTIONS

Direct the children to put up boxes for martins, bluebirds, and wrens. These may be also put up around the schoolhouses, if fortunately there is a yard with trees. Boxes for the martins should be large, containing fifteen or more compartments, each ten inches high by eight wide and eight deep, and each having a separate entrance. The martin box or house should be placed twenty feet from the ground, upon the top of a strong post or platform sustained by four smaller posts. If vines are planted at the foot of the supports, they will be ornamental and will make the houses more attractive to the birds. The English sparrows will occupy these compartments; but if the martins conclude to take possession they will push out the sparrows and their belongings without assistance. Every spring I am amused in watching the summary process of ejectment which the martins serve upon the sparrows that have taken possession of their houses. In the morning the sparrows may be in undisturbed possession, but by afternoon the martins occupy their old quarters, having pushed out the nests of the sparrows with their eggs or young.

The boxes for bluebirds and wrens should be smaller and have only one compartment. They should be nailed in the tops of trees. If the English sparrows build in them their nests should be broken up; and this repeatedly, so long as they persist in building. If this is not done the wrens and bluebirds will not come. They are incapable of coping with the sparrows.

Note when the different birds arrive in the spring, making in this way a bird calendar.

Notice also when the birds gather together into flocks in the late summer or autumn, preparatory to taking their leave. The last bird of his kind to leave should be as carefully noted as the first to arrive in your calendar. Distinguish carefully the birds of passage that stop only a short time to rest on their journeys north and south, and those that stay and help to make the summer.

You will need to make frequent excursions afield, always taking your notebook. Take first a small area and master the birds in that; then gradually extend your territory. You can take no more healthful or happy exercise. It will greatly increase the interest of children in all their school duties if their teachers make occasional bird journeys with them. Limit the size of the party to that number which will keep still as a mouse while in bird-land. Encourage the children also to make frequent excursions by themselves, in parties of three or four. Instruct them to have the sun at their backs and to carry if possible one glass with each party. Reports of these excursions can be made in school, while particular attention should be given to the exchange of the knowledge of bird haunts. This can be done during the period devoted to bird study.

Direct the party of excursionists to observe the same birds, notebook in hand, and let each one immediately put down what he actually sees. Afterward compare results. In this way improvement will be made in rapidity and accuracy of observing.

There are two ways by which birds may be closely approached. The first is to go to some locality where birds have been seen and to stand or sit in perfect quiet and wait for them to come. We have known some of the shyest wood birds to come within a few feet of the motionless observer. It is not an uncommon thing for one who waits to be able to look directly into the eyes of the American redstart, the chestnut-sided and golden-winged warbler, the wood thrush, catbird, and of almost any other of the birds.

If one can imitate the owl and make a fair "hoot," otherwise keeping still, he may attract many birds that will feel bound to settle the question of his identity. A young friend of mine, by a good imitation of a blue jay's quack, finds many little woods' folks peering at him from the trees which he might not otherwise see. The "smack" which is produced by violently kissing the back of the closed fingers will call many birds from their hiding places, especially during the nesting season. The sound is similar to that of a bird in distress.

The second method is to follow a bird very quietly and slowly, being careful not to make any motions which would startle him. In this way a shore lark has been followed all over a field, the observer gradually coming near enough to the bird to see what he was doing, and to watch his movements as he pulled the larv?of beetles out of the ground, cracked their cases, and ate the contents. All birds that feed in the fields, the meadow larks, the plovers, and the sparrows, may be studied in the same way.

It is commonly thought to be difficult to get close to the veery. On one occasion, while the writer and a companion were resting from a long ramble, the air was suddenly suffused with the songs of veeries. The music seemed to fill the woods, as an organ seems to fill the church with sound. It was weird and suggestive and never to be forgotten. The still, deep woods seemed like enchanted ground where nothing evil could come. After some search we saw one of the birds in a tree not far from us. As we approached him he flew to another tree. We humbly followed on foot from tree to tree, when to our surprise he stopped on a low tree on the outskirts of the wood and allowed us to come almost within reach of him, and to stand wonder-stricken while he sang in answer to his companions. We stayed for twenty minutes motionless. It was difficult to believe that this bird was singing. His notes had a ventriloquous effect, his beak was scarcely parted, and it was only by the trembling of the feathers of his throat that we were sure the song came from him. Since this time we have frequently found the veeries; in fact one locality is known to us as Veeryville.

It is not necessary to live in the country in order to be a bird student and to carry out the suggestions here given. All the large cities have parks where birds may be observed and be encouraged to become friendly to the observer. Central Park in New York is the home of a great variety of birds. Bronx Park is said to be a paradise for them. On Boston Common most of the birds which come to that latitude have been seen. There is no city so poor that it cannot boast of a few birds in its vicinity.

Great interest and delight may be added to the study of birds by the use of the camera. If the teacher or one of the older pupils is so fortunate as to have a kodak and will take it when visiting the woods, or will focus it upon birds in the dooryard, the pictures may possess much value. To attempt to "take" a bird in flight is, of course, a difficult matter, though it may be done; but birds upon the nest, birds feeding their young, or in the trees above the nest, evidently protecting it, have been successfully taken. Birds' nests with the eggs in make most fascinating pictures. At an entertainment given by the Pennsylvania Audubon Society in Philadelphia in December, 1898, the audience with one accord cheered the picture of a nest which was thrown upon a screen.

Work of this kind is especially adapted for high schools, and there are sure to be several painstaking amateurs among the pupils. To possess genuine value from the point of view of the naturalist, the pictures should not be touched up, no matter how much artistic beauty might thus be given to them; they should be entirely true to nature.

On no account should children be encouraged to make collections of birds or of eggs. The only objection the author has felt to the very fine bird manuals before the public is that they contain minute directions for the preparation of dead birds for purposes of mounting and preservation, and also for the collection and preservation of birds' eggs. If this were to cause the school children of the country to set out to make collections of birds and of eggs in order to study them, the study would better be omitted. Nothing more deadly than an opera glass should be aimed at a bird for a generation. The utility of a collection is not so great; a dead bird's plumage is not as beautiful as in life, and he loses every attitude and movement which makes him an individual. A corpse is not a bird. Persons who can identify birds by one glimpse of them through the trees, or by a few notes of their song, or by their flight are frequently at a loss to identify the same birds when they are dead, unless they are familiar with the dead birds.

The only collection the children should be encouraged to make is that of nests after the birds are through with them; and especially of nests with whose family history they are acquainted. These may be brought into the schoolroom. In one of our school yards the children discovered a pair of red-eyed vireos building. The nest was so situated that it could be seen from one of the upper schoolroom windows. After the young had left, the nest was taken down, and to the pleasure which the children had enjoyed in watching its builders and their family was added another. They found in the bottom of the nest little bits of the papers they had used in school with their letters and figures upon them.

VI

DIRECTIONS FOR WRITTEN WORK

Have the children give anecdotes about birds that they have observed. Let them describe actions which they saw them perform, paying particular attention to the ways of birds in eating. For example, sparrows were observed carrying hard crusts of bread to a little pool of water, formed in a dent in a tin roof, to soften before attempting to eat them. Day after day crusts were put out, and the water was renewed.

Written descriptions of birds feeding their young.--Young birds live entirely upon insect life. It has been computed that a bird during the first few weeks of its life consumes nearly one and one half times its weight of insects daily. Note the amazing amount of insect life that will be destroyed by the birds of a neighborhood in a single season. Give, if possible, illustrations from your own observation. A robin was noticed feeding one of its young, which sat on a limb with its mouth open, crying for more, except when it was stopped with food. The parent came with her beak filled with worms twenty-seven times in less than as many minutes, and then left her child seemingly as hungry as ever, for he complained and hopped along the limb, keeping a sharp lookout for several minutes. That chick must have been as full of worms as a fisherman's bait-box. Picture the condition of our lawns, gardens, and groves if all the birds were suddenly banished and the insects held full sway. In this connection, the writer should study and make quotations or abstracts from "The Birds of Killingworth," by Longfellow.

In a recent lecture, Prof. Witmer Stone, of Philadelphia, cited many facts to show that birds are nature's great check on the excess of insects, and that they keep the balance between plants and insect life. Ten thousand caterpillars, it has been estimated, could destroy every blade of grass on an acre of cultivated ground. In thirty days from the time it is hatched an ordinary caterpillar increases 10,000 times in bulk, and the food it lives and grows on is vegetable. The insect population of a single cherry tree infested with aphides was calculated by a prominent entomologist at no less than twelve million. The bird population of cultivated country districts has been estimated at from seven hundred to one thousand per square mile. This is small compared with the number of insects, yet as each bird consumes hundreds of insects every day, the latter are prevented from becoming the scourge they would be but for their feathered enemies.

Mr. E. H. Forbush, Ornithologist of the Board of Agriculture of Massachusetts, states that the stomachs of four chickadees contained 1,028 eggs of the cankerworm. The stomachs of four other birds of the same species contained about 600 eggs and 105 female moths of the cankerworm. The average number of eggs found in twenty of these moths was 185; and as it is estimated that a chickadee may eat thirty female cankerworm moths per day during the twenty-five days which these moths crawl up trees, it follows that in this period each chickadee would destroy 138,750 eggs of this noxious insect.

A pamphlet issued by the Department of Agriculture of the United States says that the cuckoo, which is common in all the Eastern States, has been conclusively shown to be much given to eating caterpillars, and, unlike most birds, does not reject those that are covered with hair. In fact, cuckoos eat so many hairy caterpillars that the hairs pierce the inner lining of their stomach and remain there, so that when the stomach is opened and turned inside out, it appears to be lined with a thin coating of hair. This bird also eats beetles, grasshoppers, sawflies, and spiders. It turns out from the investigations of the department that the suspicion with which all farmers look upon woodpeckers is undeserved by that bird. These birds rarely leave an important mark upon a healthy tree, but when a tree is affected by wood-boring larv?the insects are accurately located, dislodged, and devoured. In case the holes from which the borers are taken are afterward occupied and enlarged by colonies of ants, these ants are drawn out and eaten. Woodpeckers are great conservators of forests, and to them more than to any other agency is due the preservation of timber from hordes of destructive insects.

The department defends the much-abused crow and states that he is not by any means the enemy of the farmer, in which role he is generally represented. The pamphlet shows that he is known to eat frogs, toads, salamanders, and some small snakes, and that he devours May beetles, June bugs, grasshoppers, and a large variety of other destructive insects. It is admitted that he does some damage to sprouting corn, but this can be prevented by tarring the seed, which not only saves the corn, but forces the crow to turn his attention to insects.

Insects injurious to vegetation.--Essays may be written describing some of the insects injurious to fruit trees; also the birds that feed largely upon these insects--the warblers, thrushes, orioles, wrens, woodpeckers, vireos, and others. Tell, if possible, from your own observation, of their curious, but effective, ways of finding their food. Describe how the birds inspect the trees, limb by limb and bud by bud, in their eager search for the eggs, larv? and mature forms of insects. Note, especially, the oriole as he runs spirally round a branch to the very tip, then back to the trunk, treating branch after branch in the same way, till the whole tree has been thoroughly searched, almost every bud having been in the focus of those bright eyes. It is hard to describe which is the more beautiful--their brilliant, flaming colors or their bugle-like bursts of music. Is the woodpecker's drumming, and apparent listening with the side of his head turned to the tree, all for fun, and nothing for reward?

Birds that feed upon the potato beetle.--The grosbeaks and the tanagers. Describe these. Why are these and other brightly colored birds so shy? What has been the effect of the extensive killing of them for ornament, and the equally cruel practice of securing their young to be kept in cages? Note how much more attractive our fields and gardens would be if these beautiful beings were common in them, and by their quaint ways were "teaching us manners."

Personations of birds.--Ask the children to write "personations" of birds, as if the writer were the bird. Give them the following directions: Write in the first person. Describe yourself as accurately as you are able, without telling your name. Tell of your habits and manner of life, your summer and winter homes, your home cares--your nest building, your parental joys and anxieties, the enemies you have to avoid. Mention at some length the trouble you take to give your little ones a good start in life, and to enable them to earn their own living. Describe your songs, and try to indicate why they differ, and what you mean by each one. Try to present a somewhat complete picture of the bird and its life, from the bird's point of view. At the close of your personation the hearers may vote upon the name of the bird presented.

A family of birds may also be described, as if they were persons,--and are they not? A very fine model of this kind of work is "Our New Neighbors at Ponkapog," by T. B. Aldrich.

Have essays written upon the following subjects:--

Are there birds that do not sing?

What is the attitude of other birds to the owl?

Is any country too cold, or any too warm, for birds?

Have birds individuality?

What is the largest bird of North America?

The smallest?

What laws has your state made about birds?

Ought the "government to own" the birds? (That is, make laws for their protection.)

Is the blue jay wicked?

What birds walk?

Do birds travel at night, during their migrations?

Beginning in March, note for several days the different kinds of birds you see, which were not seen the day before. Make at least two observations daily, one in the morning and one after school. When is the greater number of new birds seen, in the morning or in the afternoon? Or, if you live in a comparatively quiet neighborhood, even in a large city, go out at night and listen for bird sounds in the air. You need not go far to make this trial--your own back door "opens into all outdoors."

What states have established a Bird Day by law?

Is woman cruel or only thoughtless?

Do robins raise more than one brood in a season? If so, do they use the same nest twice? If they raise two broods, what becomes of the first, while the mother is sitting upon the eggs for the second?

Watch for a robin leading out his family. Notice the feeding, after the birds are large enough to run and fly fairly well. The young birds are placed apart, and kept apart by the parent, who visits each one in turn, and rebukes any who tries to be piggish, sometimes rapping it with his bill when it runs out of turn. Notice this parent teaching the young to sing. It is a very interesting sight.

What birds have you heard sing at night?

More birds sing at night than is commonly supposed. The female robin calls to her mate frequently during the night, and he responds with a song. The catbird also sings at night. Last May one was heard to sing three nights in succession from eleven o'clock until daylight in response to little complaining calls from his mate. The song sparrow, warblers, and many other birds sing at night. Their songs at these times sound as if the bird were sleepy and reluctant to sing, or as if he were startled and were hurrying through the performance. Make a note of songs heard at night and try to determine the cause. Learn to distinguish the call of the female from the song of the male.

The kinds of nests.--What birds are weavers? What ones are masons or plasterers? What ones are tailors, in the construction of their nests?

Find a pair of birds engaged in nest building; robins may generally be found. Learn to distinguish the male from the female in appearance, as well as voice. Notice what materials they are using. Which bird takes the lead in building? What does the other bird do? Does he ever carry material, or does he simply act as escort? Does he ever protect his mate from other birds?

Write this out, carefully drawing your conclusions from your own observations. After the young birds have left the nest and have no further use for it, you may take the nest and examine it closely. You will find that while there is a similarity in the nests of the same kind of birds, they differ considerably in the materials of which they are composed. For example, the typical robin's nest consists of straws and hairs plastered together with mud and lined with some soft material, but others have been found made entirely of raveled rope; others of carpet rags. The bird evidently is not guided in this matter by blind instinct, but uses its reason in adapting materials that are at hand.

If you are fortunate you may find a pair of orioles building their nest. Place some bright-colored yarn or string in pieces of convenient length where the birds will see them. Some of them are almost sure to be woven into the nest. The oriole's nest may be attached to a limb by two or more cords; if it is, notice how it is prevented from swinging by side ropes. You will find it guyed against the prevailing winds. The oriole frequently ties several twigs together, and so uses these to suspend his nest. Notice the nest pouch; those built near houses are quite shallow; those near forests are much deeper. Can you tell why?

The wings of birds.--Describe the different kinds, as short and round, or long and slender, and the effect of the wing-shape upon the bird's motion in the air. Describe the flights of different birds.

Songs of birds.--Write the syllables which seem to you to express the different songs of birds. Notice the different songs of the same bird. A song sparrow was observed to have twelve different songs. He sang each one several times over, as if each song had a number of verses. Then changing his position, he would sing another. To most ears the robin's song is always the same, but close attention discovers that there are variations. Many birds are genuine musicians and compose as they sing, not having formal songs.

Free description of birds.--Write description of some bird of your acquaintance, noting the following:--

Its appearance.--Color, gait, flight, size from tip of beak to end of tail, spread of wings.

Its common name.--Why given?

Time of arrival and departure.

Character.--Is it trustful, or shy and retiring?

Song.--Season when song is most frequent, also times of day. Does it consist of many or only a few notes? Is it cheery, like the robin's, or tuneful, like the thrush's, or rollicking and rapturous, like the bobolink's, or a Romanza, like the catbird's? Notice the different emotion sounds, the notes of fear, of parental or conjugal reprimand, of joy, of anger, of deep sorrow, made by the bird at times.

Food.--Insects (kinds), seeds, fruit, etc.

Nest.--Where placed, how made?

Incidents.--From the writer's knowledge of the bird.

This bird in literature.--What writers have described, what poets have immortalized him? How did they characterize him?

Some of the following books are almost indispensable to one who wishes to know the birds:--

"Wake Robin," John Burroughs; "Birds and Poets," John Burroughs; "The Birds and Seasons of New England," Wilson Flagg; "Upland and Meadow," Charles C. Abbott; "Bird Ways," Olive Thorne Miller; "Birds through an Opera Glass," Florence A. Merriam; "Birds in the Bush," Bradford Torrey; "The Birds About Us," Charles C. Abbott; "From Blomidon to Smoky," Frank Bolles.

Recent magazines should be searched and the current ones scrutinized for articles by any of the above-named writers.

Destruction of birds.--Find out how many birds are annually slaughtered in the United States, and for what purposes.

In the report of the American Ornithologist Union published in 1886, it was estimated that about five million birds were annually required to fill the demand for the ornamentation of the hats of the American women. In 1896 it was estimated that the number thus used was ten million. "The slaughter is not confined to song-birds; everything that wears feathers is a target for the bird butcher. The destruction of 40,000 terns in a single season on Cape Cod, a million rail and reed birds (bobolinks) killed in a single month near Philadelphia, are facts that may well furnish food for reflection. The swamps and marshes of Florida are well known to have become depopulated of their egrets and herons, while the state at large has been for years a favorite slaughter ground of the milliners' emissaries." An article in Forest and Stream, speaking of the destruction of birds on Long Island, states that during a short period of four months 20,000 were supplied to the New York dealers from a single village.

The Audubon Society of Massachusetts has looked up the figures and reports that "it is proved that into England alone between 25,000,000 and 30,000,000 birds are imported yearly, and that for Europe the number reaches 150,000,000. Hence, the fashionable craze has annually demanded between 200,000,000 and 300,000,000 birds. From the East Indies alone a dealer in London received 400,000 humming birds, 6,000 birds of paradise, and 400,000 miscellaneous birds. In an auction room, also in London, within four months, over 800,000 East and West Indian and Brazilian bird skins, besides thousands of pheasants and birds of paradise, were put up for sale."

This demand for birds has been going on for a quarter of a century, and billions of rich-plumaged creatures have been slaughtered to meet it, and several of the feathered tribes have been exterminated.

Write to the following for literature upon the destruction of birds:--

Humane Education Committee, 61 Westminster Street, Providence, R. I.; George T. Angell, Boston, Mass.; Secretary of the Massachusetts Audubon Society, Boston, Mass.; Secretary of the New York Audubon Society at New York; Secretary of the Department of Agriculture, Washington, D. C.; Secretary of the Audubon Society of Pennsylvania at Philadelphia; also write to the Department of Agriculture of your own state.

VII

PROGRAMS FOR BIRD DAY

A Bird Day exercise, in order to have much value educationally, should be largely the result of the pupils' previous work, and should not be the mere repetition of a prepared program taken verbatim from some paper or leaflet. It is, of course, better to have the pupils recite this leaflet or list of statements than it would be to have it ground out of a phonograph. The program should be prepared by the pupils under direction of the teacher.

The following general suggestions are offered:--

1. For the first observance of this day by a school it would be well to have some pupil read Senator Hoar's petition of the birds to the Legislature of Massachusetts.

PETITION OF THE BIRDS

Written by Senator Hoar to the Massachusetts Legislature

The petition which was instrumental in getting the Massachusetts law passed, prohibiting the wearing of song and insectivorous birds on women's hats, was written by Senator Hoar. The petition read as follows:--

To the Great and General Court of the Commonwealth of Massachusetts: We, the song birds of Massachusetts and their playfellows, make this our humble petition. We know more about you than you think we do. We know how good you are. We have hopped about the roofs and looked in at your windows of the houses you have built for poor and sick and hungry people, and little lame and deaf and blind children. We have built our nests in the trees and sung many a song as we flew about the gardens and parks you have made so beautiful for your children, especially your poor children to play in. Every year we fly a great way over the country, keeping all the time where the sun is bright and warm. And we know that whenever you do anything the other people all over this great land between the seas and the Great Lakes find it out, and pretty soon will try to do the same. We know. We know.

We are Americans just the same as you are. Some of us, like you, came across the great sea. But most of the birds like us have lived here a long while; and the birds like us welcomed your fathers when they came here many, many years ago. Our fathers and mothers have always done their best to please your fathers and mothers.

Now we have a sad story to tell you. Thoughtless or bad people are trying to destroy us. They kill us because our feathers are beautiful. Even pretty and sweet girls, who we should think would be our best friends, kill our brothers and children so that they may wear our plumage on their hats. Sometimes people kill us for mere wantonness. Cruel boys destroy our nests and steal our eggs and our young ones. People with guns and snares lie in wait to kill us; as if the place for a bird were not in the sky, alive, but in a shop window or in a glass case. If this goes on much longer all our song birds will be gone. Already we are told in some other countries that used to be full of birds, they are now almost gone. Even the nightingales are being killed in Italy.

Now we humbly pray that you will stop all this and will save us from this sad fate. You have already made a law that no one shall kill a harmless song bird or destroy our nests or our eggs. Will you please make another one that no one shall wear our feathers, so that no one shall kill us to get them? We want them all ourselves. Your pretty girls are pretty enough without them. We are told that it is as easy for you to do it as for a blackbird to whistle.

If you will, we know how to pay you a hundred times over. We will teach your children to keep themselves clean and neat. We will show them how to live together in peace and love and to agree as we do in our nests. We will build pretty houses which you will like to see. We will play about your garden and flower beds--ourselves like flowers on wings, without any cost to you. We will destroy the wicked insects and worms that spoil your cherries and currants and plums and apples and roses. We will give you our best songs, and make the spring more beautiful and the summer sweeter to you. Every June morning when you go out into the field, oriole and bluebird and blackbird and bobolink will fly after you and make the day more delightful to you. And when you go home tired after sundown, vesper sparrow will tell you how grateful we are. When you sit down on your porch after dark, fifebird and hermit thrush and wood thrush will sing to you; and even whip-poor-will will cheer you up a little. We know where we are safe. In a little while all the birds will come to live in Massachusetts again, and everybody who loves music will like to make a summer home with you.

The signers are:--

Brown Thrasher, Robert o' Lincoln, Hermit Thrush, Vesper Sparrow, Robin Redbreast, Song Sparrow, Scarlet Tanager, Summer Redbird, Blue Heron, Humming Bird, Yellowbird, Whip-poor-will, Water Wagtail, Woodpecker, Pigeon Woodpecker, Indigo Bird, Yellowthroat, Wilson's Thrush, Chickadee, Kingbird, Swallow, Cedar Bird, Cowbird, Martin, Veery, Chewink, Vireo, Oriole, Blackbird, Fifebird, Wren, Linnet, Pewee, Phoebe, Yoke Bird, Lark, Sandpiper.

It should be noted that the result of this petition was the passage of a law by the Legislature of Massachusetts forbidding the wearing of parts of wild birds. A bill forbidding the transportation of feathers or the skins of birds from one state to another was also introduced by Senator Hoar in the United States Senate.

2. At this first exercise it would be well to have read "Our New Neighbors at Ponkapog," by T. B. Aldrich.

3. The best essays that have been written by the pupils during their preliminary study may be given. If the school has not made this preliminary study, select subjects and have essays written according to the directions already given, allowing as much time as possible for original observations.

4. Have recitations from the poets. These will add a peculiar charm to the occasion. A short list of suitable poems will be given. Many others may be found in a book called "Voices of the Speechless," published by Houghton, Mifflin & Co.

The works of John Burroughs, Bradford Torrey, Maurice Thompson, Mrs. Olive Thorne Miller, and Dr. C. C. Abbott abound in passages which are excellent for recitation. It is surprising how familiar the best-known novelists have been and are with birds. In appreciation of them they are second only to the poets. Charles Reade's description of the lark's song in the mines of Australia, in "Never Too Late to Mend," is an inspiring recitation.

5. Short quotations from well known authors should be given, if possible, by every pupil in the school. We give a few taken almost at random:--

Away over the hayfield the lark floated in the blue, making the air quiver with his singing; the robin, perched on a fence, looked at us saucily and piped a few notes by way of remark; the blackbird was heard, flute-throated, down in the hollow recesses of the wood; and the thrush, in a holly tree by the wayside, sang out his sweet, clear song that seemed to rise in strength as the wind awoke a sudden rustling through the long woods of birch and oak.--WILLIAM BLACK, in Adventures of a Phaeton.

We seemed to hear all the sounds within a great compass--in the hedges and in the roadside trees, far away in woods or hidden up in the level grayness of the clouds: twi, twi, trrrr-weet!--droom, droom, phloee!--tuck, tuck, tuck, tuck, feer!--that was the silvery chorus from thousands of throats. It seemed to us that all the fields and hedges had but one voice, and that it was clear and sweet and piercing.--WILLIAM BLACK, Ibid.

Silvia could hear the twittering of the young starlings in their nests as their parents went and came carrying food, and the loud and joyful "tirr-a-wee, tirr-a-wee, prooit, tweet!" of the thrushes, and the low currooing of the wood pigeon, and the soft call of the cuckoo, that seemed to come in whenever an interval of silence fitted. The swallows dipped and flashed and circled over the bosom of the lake. There were blackbirds eagerly but cautiously at work, with their spasmodic trippings, on the lawn. A robin perched on the iron railing eyed her curiously and seemed more disposed to approach than to retreat.--WILLIAM BLACK, in Green Pastures and Piccadilly.

A jay fled screaming through the wood, just one brief glimpse of brilliant blue being visible.--WILLIAM BLACK, Ibid.

And as they came near to one dark patch of shrubbery, lo! the strange silence was burst asunder by the rich, full song of a nightingale.--WILLIAM

BLACK, Ibid.

A sudden sound sprang into the night, flooding all its darkness with its rich and piercing melody--a joyous, clear, full-throated note, deep-gurgling now, and again rising with thrills and tremors into bursts of far-reaching silver song that seemed to shake the hollow air. A single nightingale had filled the woods with life. We cared no more for those distant and silent stars. It was enough to sit here in the gracious quiet and listen to the eager tremulous outpouring of this honeyed sound.--WILLIAM BLACK, in Strange Adventures of a House-Boat.

Shoot and eat my birds! The next step beyond, and one would hanker after Jenny Lind or Miss Kellogg.--HENRY WARD BEECHER.

There on the very topmost twig, that rises and falls with willowy motion, sits that ridiculous, sweet-singing bobolink, singing as a Roman candle fizzes, showers of sparkling notes.--Ibid.

This poet affirms that our bobolink is superior to the nightingale:--

Bobolink, that in the meadow, Or beneath the orchard's shadow, Keepest up a constant rattle Joyous as my children's prattle, Welcome to the North again, Welcome to mine ear thy strain, Welcome to mine eye the sight Of thy buff, thy black and white. Brighter plumes may greet the sun By the banks of Amazon; Sweeter tones may weave the spell Of enchanting Philomel; But the tropic bird would fail, And the English nightingale, If we should compare their worth With thine endless, gushing mirth.

--THOMAS HILL.

The mocking bird is a singer that has suffered much from its powers of mimicry. On ordinary occasions, and especially in the daytime, it insists on playing the harlequin. But when free in its own favorite haunts at night, it has a song, or rather songs, which are not only purely original, but are also more beautiful than any other bird music whatsoever. Once I listened to a mocking bird singing the livelong spring night, under the full moon, in a magnolia tree; and I do not think I shall ever forget its song.

The great tree was bathed in a flood of shining silver; I could see each twig, and mark every action of the singer, who was pouring forth such a rapture of ringing melody as I have never listened to before or since. Sometimes he would perch motionless for many minutes, his body quivering and thrilling with the outpour of music. Then he would drop softly from twig to twig till the lowest limb was reached, when he would rise, fluttering and leaping through the branches, his song never ceasing for an instant until he reached the summit of the tree and launched into the warm scent-laden air, floating in spirals, with outspread wings, until, as if spent, he sank gently back into the tree and down through the branches, while his song rose into an ecstasy of ardor and passion. His voice rang like a clarionet in rich, full tones, and his execution covered the widest possible compass; theme followed theme, a torrent of music, a swelling tide of harmony, in which scarcely any two bars were alike. I stayed till midnight listening to him; he was singing when I went to sleep; he was still singing when I woke a couple of hours later; he sang through the livelong night.--THEODORE ROOSEVELT.

Amid the thunders of Sinai God uttered the rights of cattle, and said that they should have a Sabbath. "Thou shalt not do any work, thou, nor thy cattle." He declared with infinite emphasis that the ox on the threshing-floor should have the privilege of eating some of the grain as he trod it out, and muzzling was forbidden. If young birds were taken from the nest for food, the despoiler's life depended on the mother going free. God would not let the mother-bird suffer in one day the loss of her young and her own liberty. And he who regarded in olden time the conduct of man toward the brutes, to-day looks down from heaven and is interested in every minnow that swims the stream, and every rook that cleaves the air.--DEWITT TALMAGE, D.D.

And how refreshing is the sight of the birdless bonnet! The face beneath, no matter how plain it may be, seems to possess a gentle charm. She might have had birds, this woman, for they are cheap enough and plentiful enough, heaven knows; but she has them not, therefore she must wear within things infinitely precious, namely, good sense, good taste, good feeling. Does any woman imagine these withered corpses (cured with arsenic), which she loves to carry about, are beautiful? Not so; the birds lost their beauty with their lives.--CELIA THAXTER.

I walked up my garden path as I was coming home from shooting. My dog ran on before me; suddenly he went slower and crept carefully forward as if he scented game. I looked along the path and perceived a young sparrow, with its downy head and yellow bill. It had fallen from a nest (the wind was blowing hard through the young birch trees beside the path) and was sprawling motionless, helpless, on the ground, with its little wings outspread. My dog crept softly up to it, when suddenly an old black-breasted sparrow threw himself down from a neighboring tree and let himself fall like a stone directly under the dog's nose, and, with ruffled feathers, sprang with a terrified twitter several times against his open, threatening mouth. He had flown down to protect his young at the sacrifice of himself. His little body trembled all over, his cry was hoarse, he was frightened to death; but he sacrificed himself. My dog must have seemed to him a gigantic monster, but for all that, he could not stay on his high, safe branch. A power stronger than himself drove him down. My dog stopped and drew back; it seemed as if he, too, respected this power. I hastened to call back the amazed dog, and reverently withdrew. Yes, don't laugh; I felt a reverence for this little hero of a bird, with his paternal love.

Love, thought I, is mightier than death and the fear of death; love alone inspires and is the life of all.--IVAN TOURGUENEFF.

The first sparrow of spring! The year beginning with younger hope than ever! The faint, silvery warblings heard over the partially bare and moist fields from the bluebird, the song sparrow, and the redwing, as if the last flakes of winter tinkled as they fell!--H. D. THOREAU.

I heard a robin in the distance, the first I had heard for many a thousand years, methought, whose note I shall not forget for many a thousand more,-- the same sweet, powerful song as of yore.--Ibid.

Walden is melting apace. A great field of ice has cracked off from the main body. I hear a song sparrow from the bushes on the shore,--olit, olit, olit--chip, chip, chip, che char--che wis, wis, wis. He, too, is helping to crack the ice.--Ibid.

The bluebird carries the sky on his back.--Ibid.

6. One of the most interesting features of a Bird Day program will be the personations of birds.

The following was given by a boy in the seventh grade:--

One day in February a gentleman and his wife stopped beside the wall of old Fort Marion, in St. Augustine, to listen to my song. The sun was shining brightly, and little white flowers were blooming in the green turf about the old fort. It was not time yet to build my nest, so I had nothing to do but sing and get my food and travel a little every day toward my Northern home.

I am about as large as a robin, and although there is nothing brilliant in my plumage I am not a homely bird. I like the songs of other birds and sometimes sing them. I frequently sing like my cousins, the catbirds and robins and thrushes. But I have my own song, which is unlike all the others. My mate and I build a large nest of small sticks, pieces of string, cotton, and weeds, in thick bushes or low trees. We have five eggs that are greenish blue and spotted with brown. We eat many beetles, larv? and many kinds of insects which we find feeding upon plants. The worst enemy we have is man. He steals our children almost before we have taught them to sing, and puts them in cages. He is a monster.

Many poems have been written about me. One of the finest is by Sidney Lanier, in which he calls me "yon trim Shakespeare on the tree."

Any one who has heard my song can never forget me.

What is my name?

7. Bird facts and proverbs form a valuable part of a program and may be given by some of the children. Let the pupils search for them and bring some similar to these:--

Birds flock together in hard times.

A bird in the bush is worth two in the hand.

The American robin is not the same bird as the English.

The bluebird and robin may be harbingers of spring, but the swallow is the harbinger of summer.

The dandelion tells me to look for the swallow; the dog-toothed violet when to expect the wood thrush.--JOHN BURROUGHS.

It is not thought that any one bird spends the year in one locality, but that all birds migrate, if only within a limited range.

A loon was caught, by a set line for fishing, sixty-five feet below the surface of a lake in New York, having dived to that depth for a fish.

The wood pewee, like its relative, the phoebe, feeds largely on the family of flies to which the house fly belongs.

The birds of prey, the majority of which labor night and day to destroy the enemies of the husbandman, are unceasingly persecuted.

Seventy-five per cent of the food of the downy woodpecker is insects.

The cow blackbird lays its eggs in other birds' nests, one in a nest. What happens afterwards?

Why should not a man love a bird? If the palm of one could clasp the pinion of the other, there would come together two of the greatest implements God and nature have ever given any two creatures to explore the world with, and when two bipeds gaze at each other, eye to eye, the intelligence in the one might well take off its hat to the subtle instincts in the other.--JAMES NEWTON BASKETT.

A bird on the bonnet means so much less bread on the table. A bird in the orchard is a sort of scavenger and pomologist combined, and does his share in giving you a dish of fruit for dinner. The scarlet tanager looks like a living ruby in a green tree; but--I speak bluntly--it looks like a chunk of gore on a woman's bonnet. In behalf of good taste and the birds, I enter my protest against this barbarous Custom.--LEANDER T. KEYSER.

What does it cost, this garniture of death? It costs the life which God alone can give; It costs dull silence, where was music's breath; It costs dead joy, that foolish pride may live. Ah, life, and joy, and song, depend upon it, Are costly trimmings for a woman's bonnet.

--MAY RILEY SMITH.

The program may be diversified by songs about birds. Many suitable for this occasion will be found in a collection called "Songs of Happy Life," made by Sarah J. Eddy. It is published by the Nature Study Publishing Company, of Providence, R. I.

VIII

THE POETS AND THE BIRDS

"The birds are the poets' own," says Burroughs. How could it be otherwise? The bird, with his large brain, quick circulation, and high temperature, is possessed of a tropical, ecstatic soul that blossoms into music as naturally as a bulb bursts into bloom and fragrance. He is a creature of marvelous inheritance. Poetry is a true bird-land, where you shall hear the birds as often as in any meadow or orchard on a May morning. All poets have been their lovers, from the psalmist of old, who knew "all the birds of the mountains," to our own Lowell with his "Gladness on wings--the bobolink is here."

The poets, who voice our deepest thoughts, have studied birds with the utmost care. It is astonishing to note the mention made of them in the pages of Browning, Tennyson, and in fact of every great maker of verse. Not merely as adjuncts of the landscape are they mentioned, but with intensity of feeling, as in William Watson's poem on his recovery from temporary loss of mind-- one of the most pathetic poems ever written--where he thanks the Heavenly Power for letting him feel once again at home in nature and again related to the birds and to human life. Dr. Van Dyke's wish that, when his twilight hour is come, he "may hear the wood note of the veery" finds response in the heart of every one who has listened to that song. Frequently the poet seems to have entered into the life of the bird and to have found his inner secret, as Keats in the "Ode to a Nightingale":--

Immortal bird, thou wast not born for death, No hungry generations tread thee down.

Sometimes the words seem to have caught the rhythm and ripple of the song, as in Browning's reference to the thrush:--

The wise thrush, he sings each song twice over, Lest you think he never could recapture That first fine careless rapture.

Or the bird's voice may be so suggestive as to lead the seer to the very limits of thought and aspiration, like Shelley's "Skylark." As we need the help of the naturalists, who see more accurately than we, we also need the assistance of the poet's clearer vision, with its wider and deeper sweep. How completely Sidney Lanier summed up the mocking bird! and how much more pleasing is the bird in the tree because of the bird in the poem:--

Superb and sole, upon a plumed spray That o'er the general leafage boldly grew, He summed the woods in song; or typic drew The watch of hungry hawks, the lone dismay Of languid doves when long their lovers stray, And all birds' passion plays that sprinkle dew At morn in brake or bosky avenue. Whate'er birds did or dreamed, this bird could say. Then down he shot, bounced airily along The sward, twitched in a grasshopper, made song Midflight, perched, prinked, and to his art again. Sweet science, this large riddle read me plain:-- How may the death of that dull insect be The life of yon trim Shakespeare on the tree?

Recitations from the poets should be a prominent feature of Bird Day exercises. Readings and studies of poems about birds may be very profitably made a part of the literary work of the year.

The following poems are suitable for recitation and study:--

"The Birds' Orchestra," Celia Thaxter; "The Robin," Celia Thaxter; "The Song Sparrow," Celia Thaxter; "The Blackbird," Alice Cary; "The Raven's Shadow," William Watson; "On Seeing a Wild Bird," Alice Cary; "What Sees the Owl?" Elizabeth S. Bates; "Lament of a Mocking Bird," Frances Anne Kemble; "The Snow-bird," Dora Read Goodale; "To a Seabird," Bret Harte; "The Rain Song of the Robin," Kate Upson Clark; "The Swallow," Owen Meredith; "A Bird at Sunset," Owen Meredith; "The Titlark's Nest," Owen Meredith; "The Dead Eagle," Campbell; "Ode to a Nightingale," John Keats; "What the Birds Said," John Greenleaf Whittier; "The Sandpiper," Celia Thaxter; "The Blackbird and the Rooks," Dinah Mulock Craik; "The Canary in his Cage," Dinah Mulock Craik; "The Falcon," James Russell Lowell; "The Titmouse," Ralph Waldo Emerson; "The Stormy Petrel," Barry Cornwall; "To the Skylark," Percy Bysshe Shelley; "The O'Lincoln Family," Wilson Flagg; "To a Waterfowl," William Cullen Bryant; "Robert of Lincoln," William Cullen Bryant; "The Return of the Birds," William

Cullen Bryant, "The Eagle," Alfred Tennyson; "To the Eagle," James G. Percival; "The Forerunner," Harriet Prescott Spofford; "The Skylark," James Hogg; "To the Skylark," William Wordsworth; "Sir Robin," Lucy Larcom; "The Pewee," J. T. Trowbridge; "The Yellowbird," Celia Thaxter "The Dying Swan," Alfred Tennyson; "Story of a Blackbird," Alice Cary; "The Blue Jay," Mrs. A. D. T. Whitney; "The Song Sparrow," Mrs. A. D. T. Whitney; "The Catbird," Mrs. A. D. T. Whitney; "Sparrows," Mrs. A. D. T. Whitney; "The Ovenbird," Mrs. A. D. T. Whitney; "The Vireos," Mrs. A. D. T. Whitney; "The Ovenbird," Frank Bolles; "Whip-poor-will," Frank Bolles; "The Veery," Henry Van Dyke; "The Song Sparrow," Henry Van Dyke; "The Wings of a Dove," Henry Van Dyke; "The Whip-poor-will," Henry Van Dyke; "To the Cuckoo," William Wordsworth; "Secrets," Susan Coolidge; "The Falcon," James Russell Lowell; "The Mocking Bird," Sidney Lanier; "Forbearance," Ralph Waldo Emerson; "The Mocking Bird," Clinton Scollard; "The Mocking Bird," Maurice Thompson; "The Mocking Bird," R. H. Wilde; "The Mocking Bird," A. B. Meek; "The Mocking Bird," Albert Pike; "The Song of the Thrush," Edward Markham.

This list can of course be indefinitely extended.

IN CHURCH

Just in front of my pew sits a maiden-- A little brown wing on her hat, With its touches of tropical azure, And sheen of the sun upon that.

Through the bloom-colored pane shines a glory By which the vast shadows are stirred, But I pine for the spirit and splendor That painted the wing of the bird.

The organ rolls down its great anthem; With the soul of a song it is blent; But for me, I am sick for the singing Of one little song that is spent.

The voice of the curate is gentle: "No sparrow shall fall to the ground;" But the poor broken wing on the bonnet Is mocking the merciful sound.

--Anonymous.

OBJECTS AND RESULTS OF BIRD DAY

The general observance of a "Bird Day" in our schools would probably do more to open thousands of young minds to the reception of bird lore than anything else that can be devised. The scattered interests of the children would thus be brought together, and fused into a large and compact enthusiasm, which would become the common property of all. Zeal in a genuine cause is more contagious than a bad habit.

The first Bird Day in the schools was celebrated on the first Friday in May, 1894. This is as good a date as any for the sections not in the extreme North or South.

It would better come a little after the birds begin to arrive. The afternoon session will be found sufficient to devote to the special exercises. The date should be announced some time beforehand, so that the children may prepare for it. They will not only prepare themselves, but will have the whole community aroused by the sharp points of their inquisitorial weapons. Exercises should be held in all grades, from the primary to the high school.

We quote the following from circular No. 17 sent out by the United States Department of Agriculture:--

OBJECT OF BIRD DAY

From all sides come reports of a decrease in native birds, due to the clearing of the forests, draining of the swamps, and cultivation of lands, but especially to the increasing slaughter of birds for game, the demand for feathers to supply the millinery trade, and the breaking up of nests to gratify the egg-collecting proclivities of small boys. An attempt has been made to restrict these latter causes by legislation. Nearly every State and Territory has passed game laws, and several States have statutes protecting insectivorous birds. Such laws are frequently changed and cannot be expected to accomplish much unless supported by popular sentiment in favor of bird protection. This object can only be attained by demonstrating to the people the value of birds, and how can it be accomplished better than through the medium of the schools?

Briefly stated, the object of Bird Day is to diffuse knowledge concerning our native birds and to arouse a more general interest in bird protection. As such it should appeal not only to ornithologists, sportsmen, and farmers, who have a practical interest in the preservation of birds, but also to the general public, who would soon appreciate the loss if the common songsters were exterminated.

It is time to give more intelligent attention to the birds and appreciate their value. Many schools already have courses in natural history or nature study, and such a day would add zest to the regular studies, encourage the pupils to observe carefully, and give them something to look forward to and work for. In the words of the originator of the day, "the general observance of a Bird Day in our schools would probably do more to open thousands of young minds to the reception of bird lore than anything else that can be devised." The first thing is to interest the scholars in birds in general and particularly in those of their own locality. Good lists of birds have been prepared for several of the States, and popular books and articles on ornithology are within the reach of every one. But the instruction should not be limited to books; the children should be encouraged to observe the birds in the field, to study their habits and migrations, their nests and food, and should be taught to respect the laws protecting game and song birds.

VALUE OF BIRD DAY

When the question of introducing Arbor Day into the schools was brought before the National Educational Association in February, 1884, the objection was made that the subject was out of place in the schools. The value of the innovation could not be appreciated by those who did not see the practical bearing of the subject on an ordinary school course. But at the next meeting of the Association the question was again brought up and unanimously adopted--to the mutual benefit of the schools and of practical forestry. With the advent of more progressive ideas concerning education there is a demand for instruction in subjects which a few years ago would have been considered out of place, or of no special value. If the main object of our educational system is to prepare boys and girls for the intelligent performance of the duties and labors of life, why should not some attention be given to the study of nature, particularly in rural schools where the farmers of the next generation are now being educated?

The study of birds may be taken up in several ways and for different purposes; it may be made to furnish simply a course in mental training or to assist the pupil in acquiring habits of accurate observation; it may be taken up alone or combined with composition, drawing, geography, or literature. But it has also an economic side which may appeal to those who demand purely practical studies in schools. Economic ornithology has been defined as the "study of birds from the standpoint of dollars and cents." It treats of the direct relations of birds to man, showing which species are beneficial and which injurious, teaching the agriculturist how to protect his feathered friends and guard against the attacks of his foes. This is a subject in which we are only just beginning to acquire exact knowledge, but it is none the less deserving of a place in our educational system on this account. Its practical value is recognized both by individual States and by the National Government, which appropriate considerable sums of money for investigations of value to agriculture. Much good work has been done by some of the experiment stations and State boards of agriculture, particularly in Illinois, Indiana, Massachusetts, Michigan, Nebraska, and Pennsylvania. In the United States Department of Agriculture, the Division of Biological Survey (formerly the Division of Ornithology) devotes much attention to the collection of data respecting the geographic distribution, migration, and food of birds, and to the publication and diffusion of information concerning species which are beneficial or injurious to agriculture. Some of the results of these investigations are of general interest, and could be used in courses of instruction in even the lower schools. Such facts would thus reach a larger number of persons than is now possible, and would be made more generally available to those interested in them.

If illustrations of the practical value of a knowledge of zoology are necessary they can easily be given. It has been estimated recently that the forests and streams of Maine are worth more than its agricultural resources. If this is so, is it not equally as important to teach the best means of preserving the timber, the game, and the fish, as it is to teach students how to develop the agricultural wealth of the State? In 1885 Pennsylvania passed its famous "scalp act," and in less than two years expended between $75,000 and $100,000 in an attempt to rid the State of animals and birds supposed to be injurious. A large part of the money was spent for killing hawks and owls, most of which belonged to species which were afterwards shown to be actually beneficial. Not only was money thrown away in a useless war against noxious animals, but the State actually paid for the destruction of birds of inestimable value to its farmers. During the last five or six years two States have been engaged in an unsuccessful attempt to exterminate English sparrows by paying bounties for their heads. Michigan and Illinois have each spent more than $50,000; but, although millions of sparrows have been killed, the decrease in numbers is hardly perceptible. A more general knowledge of the habits of the English sparrow at the time the bird was first introduced into the United States would not only have saved this outlay of over $100,000, but would also have saved many other States from loss due to depredations by sparrows.

Is it not worth while to do something to protect the birds and prevent their destruction before it is too late? A powerful influence for good can be exerted by the schools if the teachers will only interest themselves in the movement, and the benefit that will result to the pupils could hardly be attained in any other way at so small an expenditure of time. If it is deemed unwise to establish another holiday, or it may seem too much to devote one day in the year to the study of birds, the exercises of Bird Day might be combined with those of Arbor Day.

It is believed that Bird Day can be adopted with profit by schools of all grades, and the subject is recommended to the thoughtful attention of teachers and school superintendents throughout the country, in the hope that they will cooperate with other agencies now at work to prevent the destruction of our native birds.

T. S. PALMER,

Acting Chief of Division.

Approved:

CHAS. W. DABNEY, JR.,

WASHINGTON, D. C., July 2, 1896.

The results of Bird Day are noticeable in the schools in which it has been observed. The spirit of the schools has become fresher and brighter. There has been more marked improvement in the composition work and in the language of the pupils. Most of the children know the names of many of our birds and considerable of their ways of life, and wish to know more, and are their warm friends and protectors. The old relations between the small boy and the birds have been entirely changed. The birds themselves have been affected. They have become much more numerous. Many that were formerly rare visitants now nest freely in the shade trees of the city; for example, the orioles, the grosbeaks, the scarlet tanagers, and even the wood thrushes, and their nests are about as safe as the other homes. The children say that the birds know about Bird Day, and have come to help it along.

The correlation of the public library and the public schools is assured in those towns where Bird Day has been introduced. If there were no other result of this new day, the demand for healthful literature would be enough. The call for Burroughs and Bradford Torrey, Olive Thorne Miller, and the other writers of our out-of-doors literature is so great as to attract attention in the libraries. In fact, in one the writer knows well there is a constant and steady demand, particularly from the boys. Frank Bolles is a great favorite with them. The excursions to the woods have a new and aesthetic interest. What would Emerson have thought when he wrote that matchless bit--

Hast thou named all the birds, without a gun? Loved the wood-rose and left it on its stalk?

if he had known that the boys of another generation would be able to answer as he would have liked to have them!

The effect upon teachers is not less marked. The trip to the woods in the early morning and at sunset, sometimes with the children and sometimes in parties by themselves, has resulted in physical and mental good. A new and charming relation has sprung up between teachers and children. The tie of community of interests is a strong one. A taste in common is always conducive to friendship.

The surprising thing about this new departure in nature study is that once taken up it will never be abandoned. There is something fascinating in it. One may love trees and flowers, but their processes and habits of growth are in a way unrelated to us; but our "little brothers in feathers" are kin to us in their hopes and fears.

"When I think," said a bright woman the other day, "that this summer I have learned to know by plumage and by song twenty birds, and when I realize the delight the knowledge has given me, I feel as if I ought to go out as a missionary to the heathen women in my neighborhood." She did not exaggerate the feeling of every bird lover. So much is lost to life and good cheer by this ignorance.

Now that the Bird Day idea is being taken up and spread by the United States Government in the interests of economy, it will do much to sweeten the lives of the coming generation. The natural impulse to love and watch the birds will be encouraged instead of being disregarded.

Hast thou named all the birds, without a gun? Loved the wood-rose, and left it on its stalk? O, be my friend, and teach me to be thine!

--EMERSON.

No longer now the winged inhabitants That in the woods their sweet lives sing away, Flee from the form of man, but gather round, And prune their feathers on the hands Which little children stretch in friendly sport Towards these dreadless partners of their play.

--Extract from SHELLEY'S Queen Mab.

PART II

NOTES ON REPRESENTATIVE BIRDS

KINGBIRD (Tyrannus tyrannus)

CALLED ALSO BEE BIRD, BEE MARTIN, AND TYRANT FLYCATCHER

Length, about eight and one-half inches; spread of wings, fourteen and one-half inches. The upper parts of body are a blackish ash; top of head, black; crown with a concealed patch of orange red; lower parts pure white, tinged with pale bluish ash on the sides of the throat and across the breast; sides of the breast and under the wings rather lighter than the back; the wings dark brown, darkest towards the ends of the quills; upper surface of the tail glossy black, the feathers tipped with white.

This bird is a common summer resident of the Middle States, where it usually arrives the last of April. The name tyrannus given to it is descriptive of the character of the male, since during the breeding season he is anxious to attack everything wearing feathers. His particular aversion is hawks and crows, which he assails by mounting above his adversary and making repeated and violent assaults upon his head. He will even drive the eagle from his vicinity.

The farmer could have no better protection for his corn fields than the near-by nest of a pair of kingbirds. They eat some honeybees, but for every bee thus taken they destroy ten noxious insects. They can be easily frightened away from the vicinity of the hives without being killed.

The kingbird's nest is made of slender twigs, weed stalks, and grasses, and is placed among the branches of trees, fifteen to twenty-five feet from the ground. There are usually four or five eggs, white, spotted with brown. They have generally two broods a year.

FLICKER (Colaptes auratus)

CALLED ALSO YELLOW-HAMMER, PIGEON WOODPECKER, HITTOCK, AND YUCKER

Length, twelve and one-half inches; extent, about twelve inches. The back and wings above are of a dark umber, cross marked with streaks of black; parts surrounding the eyes, a bright cinnamon color; upper part of head, dark gray; strip of black on each side of the throat about one inch long; a narrow crescent-shaped spot of a vivid red upon the back of the head. The breast is ornamented with a broad crescent of black; under parts of the body, white, tinged with yellow, and having many round spots of black; the lower side of the wing and tail, a beautiful golden yellow; the rump, white.

This bird may be easily distinguished by the white rump and the bright yellow under the wings seen in flight.

Its food consists largely of wood lice, ants, of which it is very fond, and of other insects which it finds upon the ground or upon trees. The female differs from the male in appearance, the black strips upon the sides of the throat being very indistinct or wanting entirely.

The flicker's nest, like those of other woodpeckers, may be found in maples, oaks, apple trees, and occasionally pines or birches. They are more frequently built in clusters of trees than in exposed places, and from ten to thirty feet from the ground. The male has been noticed coming to the ground and throwing chips about, so that the nest-building might not be observed. The eggs are plain white.

RED-HEADED WOODPECKER (Melanerpes erythrocephalus)

Length, nine and one-half inches; extent, eighteen inches. The head and neck are crimson; a narrow crescent of black on the upper part of the breast; back, outer part of the wings, and tail, black glossed with blue; rump, lower part of the back, inner part of the wings, and the whole under parts, from the breast downwards, white; legs and feet, bluish green; claws, light blue. Like all woodpeckers, the tail feathers are sharp and stiff and help the bird to sustain itself upon the tree. It can strike hard blows with its bill, and drill into the hardest wood with rapidity and apparent ease. It will locate accurately the position of a grub or an insect that is within the wood of a tree, drill a hole to the inmate, and pull it out with its long, sticky tongue. The female is like the male in appearance, except that her colors are somewhat fainter. Woodpeckers as a class are beneficial, and do much to preserve trees from destructive insects.

The red-headed woodpecker builds its nest at the bottom of a tunnel in a tree, dug by other birds, or adapted to use from an already existing cavity. The nest is a mere heap of soft, decaying wood, more attention being paid by the bird to securing protection against rain than in having the nest clean and nice. The eggs are white, speckled with reddish brown, and are usually six in number.

BLUE JAY (Cyanocitta cristata)

Length, twelve inches; extent, seventeen inches. The head is crested; crest and upper back are a light purplish blue; wings and tail, bright blue; a collar of black proceeds from the hind part of the head, gracefully curving down each side of the neck to the upper part of the breast, where it forms a crescent; the chin, throat, and under parts are white or slightly tinged with blue; the tail is long and composed of twelve feathers marked with cross curves of black, each feather being tipped with white, except the two middle ones, which are a dark purple at the ends. The legs and bill are black.

The nest of the blue jay is large and clumsily made, and is placed high in the branches of tall trees, the cedar being preferred. It is lined with fine, fibrous roots. The eggs are four or five in number, of a dull olive, spotted with brown.

BOBOLINK (Dolichonyx oryzivorus)

CALLED ALSO RICEBIRD, REEDBIRD, AND BOBLINCOLN

Length, seven and one-fourth inches; extent, twelve and one-fourth inches. The female is a little smaller than the male. The male has the top and sides of the head and under parts black; large yellowish patch on the back of the neck; middle of back is streaked with buff; lower part of the back and upper tail feathers, grayish white; wings and tail, black; the bill is short, conical, and is blue black. The tail feathers are sharp-pointed and stiff like a woodpecker's. The female has the upper parts olive buff streaked with black; yellowish beneath; two stripes on the top of head; wings and tail, brownish; tail feathers with pointed tips. In the autumn the male puts on a dress similar to that of the female, the colors being a little more pronounced.

The nest is built on the ground, of grasses. It contains from four to seven grayish eggs, spotted with blotches of brown.

RED-WINGED BLACKBIRD (Agelaius phoeniceus)

CALLED ALSO AMERICAN REDWING, MARSH BLACKBIRD, AND SWAMP BLACKBIRD

Length, nine and one-half inches; spread of wings, fifteen and one-fourth inches. The male is of a uniform black, which glistens in the sunshine; shoulders bright scarlet bordered with brownish yellow; bill, legs, and feet black. The female is smaller than the male, and differs greatly from him in appearance. She is dark brown above, streaked with lighter and darker shades; below, gray streaked with brown; throat and edge of wing tinged with pink or yellow, but mostly pink in the summer. The young male at first resembles the female, but may soon be recognized by black feathers appearing in patches.

The nests, which are composed chiefly of coarse grasses lined with finer grass, are built upon the ground or in low bushes. Those built in bushes are compact, the others are generally loosely made. The eggs number four to six, spotted and lined with black and brown.

MEADOW LARK (Sturnella magna)

CALLED ALSO FIELD LARK

Length of male, ten and one-half inches; spread of wings, sixteen inches. The female is smaller. The feathers above are dark brown, with transverse dark brown bars across the wings and tail; the outer tail feathers, white; the throat, breast, under parts and edge of wing, bright yellow. A yellow spot extends from the nostril to the eye. The breast has a large black crescent, the points of which reach halfway up the neck; hind toes long, its claws twice as long as the middle one. The female is like the male, but duller in color.

Their food is various forms of insects, beetles, grasshoppers, cutworms, larv?

sometimes varied by the seeds of grasses and weeds, wild cherries, and berries.

The nest is built upon the ground, of dried grasses, carefully concealed in tufts of grass. The eggs are oval, usually five in number; they are white, dotted with reddish brown. Both sexes engage in building the nest.

BALTIMORE ORIOLE (Icterus galbula)

CALLED ALSO GOLDEN ROBIN, FIREBIRD, AND HANGBIRD

Length, about eight inches; extent, twelve and one-half inches. The head, throat, and upper part of the back are black; the lower part of the back, the breast, and forward part of the wing are a brilliant orange. The base of the middle tail feathers is orange, the ends black; all the others are orange, with a black band in the middle. The female is smaller, and colors are not so bright.

The nest is composed of various materials, such as grasses, plant fibers, hairs, strings, which are capable of being interwoven. It is suspended near the end of a limb. The eggs are commonly five in number. They are whitish and variously marked with black and brown spots and lines.

SONG SPARROW (Melospiza fasciata)

Length, a little over six inches; extent, about eight and one-half inches. General color of the upper parts brown streaked with black, gray, and different shades of brown; no white wing bars; the crown dull brown, with a faint grayish line in the middle; white line over the eye; under parts whitish with numerous dark brown streaks on the neck, breast, and sides; a conspicuous black spot in the middle of the breast; bill, legs, and feet are brownish. The female is the same as the male.

The nest is composed of grasses, lined with finer grass. It is built in a low bush or on the ground. The eggs vary greatly both in size and in markings.

They are generally five in number, and are greenish or bluish white, variously spotted with brown. These birds raise two and sometimes three broods.

Not to know the song sparrow is to miss one of the delights of summer.

GOLDFINCH (Spinus tristis)

CALLED ALSO YELLOWBIRD, THISTLE-BIRD, AND WILD CANARY

Length, five and one-fourth inches; extent, nearly nine inches. The back and under parts are bright yellow; wings and crown cap, black; tips of the wing and tail feathers, white on their inner webs. The male in autumn loses his black cap, and his bright yellow parts change to a dull brownish yellow similar to the female; the wings and tail, however, remain darker and the white markings are more noticeable than those of the female. The female has no black cap; the wings and tail are dusky, marked with white as in the male; lower parts, yellowish gray; upper parts inclining to olive.

The nest is cup-shaped, composed of plant fibers, lined with downy substances. The eggs are usually five in number, white or faintly bluish.

ROSE-BREASTED GROSBEAK (Habia Ludoviciana)

Length, eight inches; extent, thirteen inches. Back, throat, and head are black; breast and under wings, rose-red; wings, black; rump, white tipped with black. The female is about the same size as the male. Her upper parts are brown, margined with buff and pale brown, with whitish line over the eye; wings and tail, dark gray; feathers of the fore wing tipped with white; under parts yellowish, streaked with brown.

The nest is a thin, flat structure made of dried grasses and small twigs. The eggs are greenish white with brown spots; they are usually four in number. These birds are said to be great destroyers of potato bugs.

CEDAR BIRD (Ampelis cedrorum)

CALLED ALSO CHERRY BIRD, AMERICAN WAXWING, AND CANADIAN ROBIN

Length, seven and one-fourth inches; extent, about twelve inches. The head is crested; general color, grayish brown; forehead, chin, and a line through the eye, black; tail and wings, gray; tail tipped with yellow; some of the shorter wing feathers are tipped with small oblong beads of red, resembling sealing wax.

These birds are fond of cherries and berries. The fruit grower can protect his interests by planting some choke cherries, mulberries, and mountain ash trees at the edges of his orchard. Cedar birds destroy great quantities of insects, and are entitled to a part of the fruit which they have helped to save.

The nest is large and loosely made of strips of bark, leaves, grasses, sometimes of mud, lined with finer materials. The eggs are usually five in number, dull gray spotted with black and brown.

BROWN THRUSH (Harporhynchus rufus)

CALLED ALSO BROWN THRASHER

Length, eleven and one-fourth inches; extent, thirteen inches; tail, five and one-half inches long. The iris is yellow; upper parts, reddish or cinnamon brown; lower parts, white; feathers of middle wing edged with white; the breast and sides strongly spotted with dark brown.

The nest is a carelessly made, bulky affair, composed of rootlets, strips of bark, twigs, leaves, and other material. It is generally poorly concealed in some low tree or even in the corner of a fence. For this reason it is frequently broken up. The eggs, four or five in number, are brownish mottled with darker brown. During the nesting season the bird at morning and in the afternoon ascends to the tops of trees and pours forth his wonderful song. He has even been thought to be "showing off," for he will sing almost as long as any one will stay to listen; but he is probably attracting attention to himself in order to detract it from his nest, which is always somewhere within the circle of his song.

CHICKADEE (Parus atricapillus)

CALLED ALSO BLACKCAP TITMOUSE

Length, five and one-half inches; extent, eight inches. The general color of back is ashy; the top of head, throat, and chin black; no crest; under parts, whitish with buff on the sides; wing and tail feathers edged with white; legs, bluish gray; bill, black. The song of this bird is an oft-repeated chick-a-dee, from which it takes its name. Its call consists of two high notes, the first one a third above the second, which may be easily imitated, and the bird attracted to the vicinity of the person answering his call.

Its nest is made of grasses and feathers, placed in a hole in a stump or tree; frequently in the deserted cavity made by a woodpecker. The eggs, six or seven, are white, spotted with brown about the larger end.

CATBIRD (Galeoscoptes Carolinensis)

Length, nine inches; extent, eleven and one-half inches. The general color is dark slate, somewhat lighter beneath; top of the head and tail, black; under side of tail near the base, chestnut; bill and feet, black; eye, brown. The female is like the male, but smaller. As a musician, this bird closely approaches the brown thrush. There are great differences in individual singers.

The nest is bulky, composed of twigs, rootlets, dead leaves, strips of bark, etc. Strips of grapevine bark are quite commonly used, some nests being constructed almost wholly of this material. The eggs are generally four in number and of a greenish blue, unmarked.

BLUEBIRD (Sialia sialis)

Length, six and one-half inches; extent, twelve and one-half inches. The upper parts, wings, and tail are bright blue; sides of the head and upper part of chin also blue; throat, breast, and sides, reddish brown; abdomen and under side of tail, white; legs and bill, blackish; eye, brown. The female is similarly marked, but the colors are duller.

The bluebird's song is a continued pleasing, rich warble.

The nest is loosely built of grasses, feathers, and soft material, in holes of trees, in hollows of posts, or in bird boxes. The eggs are light blue and are four or five in number.